INTRODUCTION

Of the many popular pets that you can choose from, the golden hamster, *Mesocricetus auratus*, is unusual. Unlike the rabbit, guinea pig, mouse, or rat, it is a relative newcomer to the pet scene, yet it has gained a tremendous following within a comparatively short period wherever pets are kept. While the other pets mentioned, along with the gerbil, are social animals that live happily in small groups, the hamster is very much a loner by nature. In this respect, it compares to one of the newest animals on the pet scene: the hedgehog.

BRIEF HISTORY

The golden hamster is but one of 24 species of hamster that are found in the Old World from Europe to Asia and China. It was first imported into England during the 19th century. The stock seems to have died out around 1910 without having created any great impact. Around 1930, a small group of these little rodents was imported into Palestine from Mount Aleppo in Syria. A breeding colony was established after a rather unsuccessful start, and examples were sent around the world to laboratories and zoos. Included among the zoos was London Zoo. It is thought that many of the present numerous lines of pet hamsters around the world derive from stock initially bred at that zoo.

Hamsters are cute and active animals that have become a leading household pet.

The hamster first arrived in the US around 1938, but this cute little mammal did not really make any great impact on the pet world until the late 1940s and early 1950s. It then took off in a big way and has remained extremely popular ever since. In 1971, a small group of these animals was imported into the US, possibly the first fresh bloodlines since the original captives of 1930! Examples of the closely related Brandt's hamster were imported into the US in 1965 and 1971.

COLORS AND COAT TYPES

The basic color pattern of the wild golden hamster is shades of red-brown on the back and flanks, with a white or cream underbelly. Some specimens have a distinct black striping on the back and sides. From this basic color arrangement, there have appeared a number of major color mutations which, in recombination, have resulted in over 30 varieties from which you can choose.

There are four coat types. The original wild type coat is short, but mutations have given rise to the long-haired, the satin, and the rex. In theory, you thus have over 120 varieties to choose from, though at this time every color and pattern is not available in every coat type.

Apart from the accepted colors and patterns, there is an almost unlimited number of subtle shades and variably marked individuals that are every bit as pretty, sometimes much more so, than the recognized varieties. This wealth of colors and patterns is one reason why the hamster enjoys such a strong following. Many hobbyists specialize in color breeding. There is also a well-organized show system for hamsters, so the hobby offers something for all types of enthusiasts.

HAMSTERS IN THE WILD

The hamster is a small mammal with a size of about 13cm (5 in.) and a typical weight of around 115g (4 oz). The female is usually somewhat larger and heavier than the male. However, this is a relative matter, so it is not the basis for sex determination. The tail is short, about 1.5cm ($^1/_2$ in.) in length. Hamsters live solitary lives in small burrows and come together only for the purpose of reproduction. In regard to activity level, these animals are basically nocturnal, but they may venture forth during daylight hours.

Their natural habitat is dry areas that are rocky and/or well shrubbed. The diet is omnivorous, consisting of roots, plants, seeds, invertebrates, and any meaty carrion that may come their way as they forage. They possess expandable cheek pouches capable of holding quite large quantities of food, which is cached for consumption at a later time. If the weather gets very cold, or food is scarce, hamsters will become torpid and enter a short hibernation of up to 28 days. Some species will go into torpor for just a few days, wake up to feed on their stored food, then go back to sleep, and repeat the process. The lifespan is relatively short at two to three years. It may be somewhat longer if the individual has hibernated frequently.

THE BASIS OF POPULARITY

Hamsters have become popular for a number of reasons. Possibly one of the most obvious is that unlike gerbils, mice, and rats (their logical pet competitors), they have virtually no tail; this gives them greater appeal to many people. They are quiet, almost odorless, and have a cute facial

A female dominant spot hamster. Hamsters can make wonderful pets for people of all ages.

expression. They are easy to care for in respect to housing and food and, as discussed, are seen in a very extensive range of colors and patterns. Once they are hand tame, they become very friendly little pets that are inexpensive to purchase. They are reliable breeders and a whole hobby has been built up around them.

In the following chapters, everything you need to know about housing, care, and generally enjoying these desirable little rodents is discussed.

Hamsters are popular pets because they are inexpensive, tame, and come in a variety of colors and coats.

Hamsters have a tendency to store food in a particular area of the cage. Too much stored food can attract insects into the area so keep this in mind when cleaning.

A female golden hamster. A healthy hamster has bright eyes, is alert, and is interested in its surroundings.

ACCOMMODATIONS

Of all the small pets, the hamster has received the most specific consideration in regard to its accommodations. Indeed, it is the only one that can be provided with commercial housing that resembles its housing in the wild. Most rodents are housed in metal cages, a number of which are designed for hamsters. The obvious alternatives are an aquarium or any of the tube systems that were quite an innovation when they appeared some years ago. The use of wooden cages for hamsters is not recommended because they are more difficult to keep clean, and these pets are experts at gnawing exit holes into them!

THE AQUARIUM

An aquarium makes an ideal home for a hamster. It has the advantage that it is available in a range of sizes from small to very large, and, when fitted with a wire top duly weighted down, is escape proof. A large aquarium is rather costly; but when fitted with some plastic tubes and shelves, it is really the ultimate in hamster housing.

CAGES

Commercially made cages may be all metal, or they may have a metal top that clamps onto a plastic base. The latter are better because they do not rust, which metal bases are apt to do with

Your pet shop will have many hamster cages available. Remember to clean the cage on a regular basis.

Fresh water must be readily available to hamsters at all times as hamsters can dehydrate in a short period of time.

wear and the effect of the hamster's urine. The weld wire bars should be chromium plated for long life and ease of cleaning. It is always best to obtain the largest cage you can afford. This offers your pet more room to exercise in, and offers you more scope to include various accessories that will make its life more interesting. Some cages come complete with a small raised platform on which there is a nestbox reached via a ladder. Other cages come without fittings, which you, of course, must provide. For the unfurnished cage, you should obtain a plastic or metal nestbox, an exercise wheel, preferably the solid type rather than those with open metal treads), one or two small crock pots, and an automatic water dispenser. All of these items are available in a range of styles from any good pet shop. You can add a few items that your hamster will enjoy. A wooden bobbin is always of interest to your pet, as is a plastic tube in which it can scamper in and out. A few large pebbles in one corner will provide something upon which it can clamber. One or two pieces of fruit tree branches will be useful for your pet to gnaw on and gain nutritious fibrous material in the process.

An ideal home for a hamster. Cages are important not only to keep your hamster in but also to feel secure from any predators that may abound. Make sure the top is on correctly so that your hamster does not escape.

THE TUBE SYSTEM

There are now a number of variations on this interesting method of housing hamsters. Basically, they comprise a number of tubes that are connected to large tub-like structures that are used as nests, toilets, and general eating areas. The great advantage of these systems is that you can start with a basic kit and then keep adding on. You can create a very interesting miniature tunnel system that equates to the home

FLOOR COVERING

The most popular material for covering your hamster's floor is white wood shavings. Alternatives are granulated paper sold in pet shops, natural plant litter sold for cats (not clay litter, which is abrasive), or possibly potting soil. Garden soil is not recommended because it may contain the eggs of parasites, while sand is abrasive and can cause irritation to your pet. For bedding, you can use wood shavings, strips of paper, or one of the synthetic fibers sold for

A really good exercise apparatus for your hamster is a wheel. Hamsters will take advantage of this and run for hours on end.

of the hamster in the wild. The tubes are made of clear plastic so that you can watch your pet as it moves around the series of tunnels and dens.

The only cautionary note with these tubes is that a large and overweight hamster just might get stuck occasionally! Do keep an eye on your pet as it travels through the tunnels so that you are sure it has no problems.

rodent nests. Do not use wood wool because it can get tangled around your hamster's feet or neck. Hay is used by many hobbyists because it is soft and edible. However, its drawback is that even good quality hay may contain fungal spores and parasites that will flourish in the warm and sometimes damp (from urine) conditions created in a nestbox.

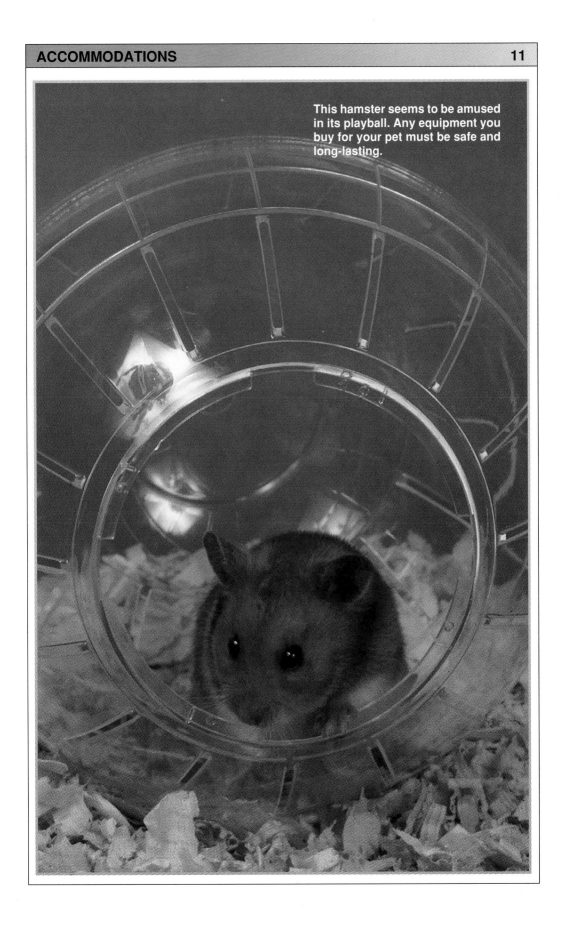

This hamster seems to be amused in its playball. Any equipment you buy for your pet must be safe and long-lasting.

LOCATION OF THE CAGE

It is important that you select the location for your pet's home with care. It should not be placed where it might be exposed to a draft, such as opposite a door. Nor should it be placed where it will be subject to the direct rays of the sun for any length of time. Likewise, do not place it over or near a radiator that is constantly going off and on. This will result in sudden temperature fluctuations that are not healthy for any pet.

The cage needs to be placed at a convenient height so that you can easily attend to cleaning chores without having to bend over. At the same time, you will more readily be able to watch your pet's activities if it is on a table or shelf.

HANDLING YOUR HAMSTER

It is important that your hamster is handled gently and on a day-to-day basis. This way, it will become very tame and a joy to own. If it was a youngster when purchased, it should already be at least familiar with being picked up. Be aware that a hamster can inflict a painful bite if it is not tame, so attend to this matter sooner rather than later, and before young children are allowed to hold the pet. Do not use gloves because they will not impart the scent and feel of your hand. You also lose a certain degree of sensitivity when wearing gloves and may hold the pet too tightly, thus prompting it to wriggle and try to bite. If your pet displays aggression, you can always use your thumb and index finger to

Hamsters need ample time to adjust to their new environments. It's a good idea to buy your equipment before you purchase a hamster.

Hamsters will bite on occasion so anyone who handles your pet should be cautioned accordingly.

grasp the loose skin on its neck to lift it, then place it on your hand. As it comes to know that you mean it no harm, you will be able to "cup" it by sliding your fingers under its body and lifting it. It will enjoy climbing up your arm and onto your shoulder if you are sitting in an arm chair.

SECURITY WHEN OUT OF ITS HOME

Never leave your hamster out of its accommodations and unattended; otherwise, it will soon disappear under a sofa, behind a heavy appliance, into a crack in your floorboards, or in some other equally difficult-to-get-at location.

Needless to say, it must never be allowed to roam in a room that contains a cat or a dog— otherwise, it may quickly be an ex pet!

Should it by chance escape in a room, you should leave its cage near to where you think it is. It may enter the cage for food and remain there because it may have frightened itself on its travels.

If this fails, another ploy may work. Place a small bucket in the room and line the base with a towel or shavings. Put some enticing edibles, such as pieces of apple and favored seeds, into the bucket.

Now build a non-skid ramp using a length of wood on which have been placed one or two tidbits. With luck, your pet will follow the trail of goodies until it reaches the top of the bucket, where it may drop/jump in to get at the main course!

ROUTINE CLEANING

If you do not want your pet's accommodations to become smelly, and in order to keep the hamster in good health, the housing must be thoroughly cleaned every week. Remove and dispose of all floor covering and bedding material. Wash the cage base and the metal bars with bleach. Rinse them and allow them to dry before adding the floor covering and nestbox material. Pots should be washed daily, and the water bottle should be washed weekly.

If you keep a number of hamsters, you should organize the cages and number each one of them. The cage furnishings, food pots, and exercise wheels should be numbered to match. This way, you minimize the risk that pathogens can be transferred directly from cage to cage via the furnishings.

Hamsters enjoy all kinds of toys and home furnishings. However, they need lots of room to exercise so don't overcrowd the cage with them.

White wood shavings make the best bedding material. You may want to provide more in the area where your hamster sleeps.

CHOOSING A HAMSTER

Given the fact that hamsters are not very long lived (two to three years average), it is important that you obtain a very healthy youngster. This is your main priority. Other factors that you will need to consider are which sex is preferred, and, of course, the color, pattern, and coat type that you favor.

PURCHASE AGE

Baby hamsters are weaned when they are about 21 days of age, so anytime after this is the time to obtain one. Four to eight weeks of age is ideal because they should be very independent and eating well by this time. Although youngsters can live together amicably until they are about eight weeks of age, it is best to separate them once they pass the six-week mark. If this is not done, they may start fighting, while the females may become pregnant. Each pet should have its own accommodations. Do not mix hamsters with other small rodents, such as mice or gerbils, thinking they will be company for each other. Hamsters are solitary by nature and will not welcome any other pet into their domain.

SELECTING A HEALTHY PET

When purchasing any pet, your first observations should be of the

When purchasing a hamster, be certain you choose one that has a clean coat with no bald patches.

Choose a reputable source when purchasing a hamster. You should be able to pay a reasonable price for the quality of hamster you intend to raise.

conditions under which the pet is living. If they are not very clean, with water and food not in evidence, and the pets are cramped together in a small cage, you should make a hasty retreat and find another supplier. If the overall conditions are satisfactory, request confirmation from the pet shop assistant that the stock on view is of the desired young age.

Select one or two that are of appealing color and the sex wanted, and then check them for health. The eyes should be round, wide open and clear, with no signs of weeping or staining of the fur around them. The nose should be dry to just moist, never runny. The nostrils should show no signs of being swollen.

If you can see the teeth, this is all for the good. The top incisors should just overlap, but touch, those of the lower jaw. In this way, the teeth will wear evenly against each other. If the alignment is incorrect, the incisors will continue growing and create problems for the pet—this condition is known as malocclusion and is very undesirable. Inspect the anal region for any signs of diarrhea. Some strains of hamsters are especially prone to a disease known as wet tail, or regional enteritis. It is invariably fatal (about 48 hours) to youngsters of 3-8 weeks of age. Other clinical signs of this problem will be anorexia, dehydration, and general disinterest (depression) in what is going on around the individual. It is highly contagious.

Check the fur by parting it against its lie. There should be no signs of external parasites (fleas or lice), which would suggest dirty

CHOICE OF SEX

It does not matter which sex you obtain. You can establish which sex is which by inspecting the ano-genital region. In the male, the distance between the anus and the genitals is greater

If you want a tame hamster, you must handle it as often as possible. Be careful not to drop the animal or give it the opportunity to escape.

living conditions. Be sure there are no bald areas of fur, which may be caused by ringworm, a fungal disease not readily eradicated. There must be no lumps or other abrasions anywhere on the body. The hamster has five digits on each foot, but a missing claw is no major problem as long as it has healed cleanly. Finally, it is better to start off with a pet that shows no resentment at being handled than one which does.

than that in the female, where the two openings are quite close together. The female mammae vary in number from 12 to 17, with 14 (7 pairs) being typical. Generally, the female is somewhat larger than the male. The latter sex has small scent glands, which release a characteristic odor—but this is not such as to make the female superior on this account.

COLOR, PATTERN, AND COAT TYPE

The potential range of colors

A light golden male hamster. It shouldn't make a difference which sex to obtain. Both sexes make equally fine companions.

This is not the correct way to handle a hamster. The proper procedure is to cradle it in the palms of your hands rather than grasp it. This will also minimize injuries due to falls.

and patterns in hamsters is quite bewildering. Unless you have a very definite idea of what you want, it is best to select a healthy pet that displays a friendly disposition, rather than a well-marked individual of dubious health and nature. But if you do have a definite idea of what you want, then be prepared to wait until just the right individual can be located. Visit a number of pet shops and see who generally has the largest selection of stock.

having to purchase what is available at the store at the time of the hamster's purchase. The pet shop will supply a small cardboard box in which you can transport hammy home. However, if the journey is lengthy, it is best to take a cake or cookie tin, which your new pet will not be able to nibble on. Pierce a few air holes in the lid and line the tin with white wood shavings and maybe some nesting material. Scatter some dry food on the bottom and include

A properly tamed hamster will love to get attention once it has become used to its new home.

BRINGING YOUR HAMSTER HOME

It is always preferable that you purchase your hamster's accommodations in advance of obtaining the pet. This enables you to shop around so that you can buy exactly the sort of housing you want, rather than

one or two slices of apple or a similar fruit, from which your pet can derive moisture. Make the homeward trip direct, rather than stopping to shop or visit friends. Once at home, put the hamster in its new house and leave it alone for 24 hours so that it can

Above: Active hamsters, such as this one, are alert and playful. Avoid obtaining hamsters that seem listless and lethargic. *Below*: Hamsters are known to be curious. They will examine and look around for anything that is within reach.

investigate and generally settle down, have a meal, and a night's sleep. The next day you can begin the process of bonding your pet to you and other family members.

As far as IQ level, hamsters may not compare to cats, dogs, or parrots; nonetheless, they are quite intelligent, as are most rodents. They will certainly become familiar with your body scent and the way you handle them. If this is always gentle, you will be rewarded with a very friendly pet. Be sure that they are never left to waddle along table tops and similar furnishings because they display little fear of heights. They could easily fall and injure themselves badly in the process. Always supervise young children with these pets until you are quite satisfied that they understand how to handle them gently.

FEEDING

Hamsters are omnivorous in their feeding habits, which means that they will eat foods of both plant and animal origin. This having been said, they have a strong leaning toward being plant eaters (herbivorous), so this should be reflected in their feeding regimen. Always try to supply your pet with a wide-ranging diet, as this is your best insurance that no important constituents are missing.

FOOD COMPOSITION

All foods contain proteins, fats, carbohydrates, vitamins, minerals and water. Each of them serves its own purpose in body metabolism.

Proteins are used to build body tissues. They are essential for a hamster that is growing, breeding, or recovering from illness. An excess of proteins results in greater layers of fat. This is not only wasteful of these more costly ingredients but also is obviously not good for your pet's health. Examples of protein-rich foods include meat, poultry, fish, butter, eggs, cheese, milk, and seeds such as peanut, pine nut, safflower, and sunflower.

Fats provide insulation against cold weather and are a readily available reserve source of energy. They are the substances that give food its taste. Any food that is rich in protein invariably has a moderate to high fat content.

Carbohydrates are the main foods that provide energy for day-to-day muscular activity. They are composed of both simple and compound sugars that can quickly be oxidized in the body to release their stored energy. They are the least expensive of all foods. Carbohydrates include grain crops (wheat, barley), most seeds, and their byproducts (bread, breakfast cereals, dog biscuits).

It is important to not overfeed your hamster. Uneaten food will be stale and eventually sour over a few days.

Vitamins are not really foods but chemical compounds that are crucial to good health. They enable chemical reactions within body cells to take place. There are a number of vitamins, some of which can be synthesized in the body, some of which cannot and must be provided in the diet. If your pet eats a wide-ranging diet, then it is unlikely to ever suffer from vitaminosis, which is a lack of one or more important vitamins.

The reverse of this is hypervitaminosis, meaning an

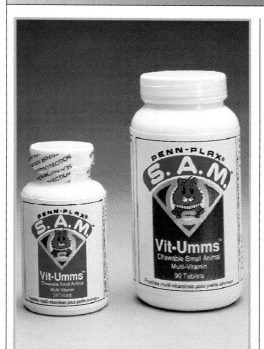

Above: Vitamins play an important role in your hamster's life. Chewable multivitamins are available at your local pet shop. Photo courtesy of Penn Plax.

Below: The best way to keep your hamster healthy is to feed it a variety of foods.

excess of these compounds. This is as dangerous as a lack of them, so only provide vitamin supplements if your pet eats a very restricted diet, and then only under veterinary recommendation. Vitamin-rich foods include fruits, green plants and certain vegetables, fish-liver oils, and wheat germ. Each of these contains differing quantities of given vitamins, as do all foods.

Minerals are natural elements such as iron, copper, magnesium, potassium, phosphorus, selenium and calcium. Lack of them can result in poor cell structure and problems in normal body functions. An excess of some minerals can disrupt the absorption of other minerals as well as the absorption of vitamins. However, these extremes are unlikely in a hamster that eats a typical well-balanced diet.

Water is the elixir of life and without it no living creature can survive indefinitely. Fruits and plant matter are the richest source of water. Regardless of whether or not your hamster is eating dry or moist foods, it should have access to water at all times. A pet lacking enough water will quickly start to lose good health.

A SUGGESTED FEEDING PROGRAM

There are two basic ways in which you can feed your hamster. One is by purchasing ready-mixed bags of hamster food, some of which have already been fortified with essential vitamins. The other is by making up meals from the various constituents required. The ideal program will utilize both. This will provide a wide-ranging menu that has good content as well as taste appeal.

The hamster foods sold in pet shops will contain grain crops (crushed oats, barley, wheat, etc), formulated rabbit pellets, sunflower seed, crushed dog biscuit, and other dried plant matter.

You can supply fresh fruits and vegetables chopped into small pieces, plus a little cheese, yogurt, or other high-protein foods already discussed. Do not overdo the protein foods—offer just enough to add extra taste to the meal.

The fruits and vegetable items can include apple, plum, grape, carrot, celery, spinach, indeed the list is extensive. It is a case of trying a number of items and seeing which have the greatest appeal. Always wash fruits and vegetables before you feed them to your pet, as they may contain residual chemicals from crop spraying. Wild plants can be given as well. Examples are dandelion, chickweed, clover, plantain and parsley. Never feed plants that are grown from bulbs, nor any other plant that you are unsure of—*if in doubt, leave it out* is a good philosophy.

You can grow your own greens for your hamster. Pet shops sell greenhouse kits that provide everything you need to grow fresh organic greens. Photo courtesy of Four Paws.

WHEN TO FEED AND HOW MUCH

It is necessary to feed your pet only once per day if the correct amount of food is supplied. The meal should be given in the early evening, which coincides with the natural activity level of these pets. The important point is to feed your hamster at the same time each day.

The amount of food required is variable and determined on an individual basis that is influenced by the following factors.

1. Age of hamster. A young growing pet will eat more than an older fully mature specimen.
2. Ambient temperature of the hamster's environment. The warmer it is the less the pet will eat because it does not need extra layers of fat.
3. Activity level. A pet that has ample room for exercise will consume more than a pet kept in small accommodations.
4. State of health. A normal fit specimen will have a larger appetite than one which is not feeling very well.
5. Breeding state. A breeding female will require progressively more food as she nears pregnancy than will a non-breeding female.
6. Quality of food. The better the quality the less will be consumed, as the better foods will be richer in their content.

Keeping all of these factors in mind, the best way to establish individual needs is by trial and error. Put a quantity of dried foods into your pet's dish and see how much is consumed at a single sitting. Do likewise with a selection of moist foods, including high-protein foods. Adjust the next meal up or down according to whether or not any food was left. As a guide, there should be some dried foods left; but you do not want moist foods left out much over a couple of hours, or they will start to sour. This is especially so in warm weather.

It is important to remember that hamsters fill their cheek pouches with food and take it to their nestbox to eat later. Check the nest box every two to three days to see how much, if any, food has been stored.

You should always watch your pet when it eats so that you know which foods are the preferred items. They are the ones that will be consumed first, so an order of preference can be determined. This may be useful to know if your pet is feeling unwell, when you can then give it extra of its favorite foods to encourage it to eat.

Hamsters must have water available at all times. The most convenient way of accomplishing this is to supply your hamster's house with a water bottle. Photo courtesy of Penn Plax.

BREEDING AND EXHIBITION

Although hamsters are reliable and prolific breeders, you should not contemplate entering this side of the hobby without giving the matter serious thought. Breeding takes up a lot more time than does owning one or two pets. There is then the added cost, and space, of extra housing that will be required. The breeding stock and their offspring will, of course, mean an increase in the amount of money that you spend on food.

START OFF RIGHT

If you are determined to become a breeder, you should try to make things as favorable for yourself as you can. This is achieved in the following manner.

1. Start on a small scale. This is a prudent policy anyway because many people start with great enthusiasm and then lose interest within a year or so.
2. Start by spending the extra cash needed in order to get quality breeding stock from a breeder/exhibitor who has a winning stud of hamsters.
3. Enter your youngsters into hamster shows so that you gain a reputation as an exhibitor.
4. Most important of all, be sure your main objective is to breed for quality and health. Never compromise on these qualities in favor of quantity.
5. Find the time to study basic principles of genetics. This will

Hamster shows do exist, but they are not as common as other animal exhibitions. Contact your nearest hamster club to find out all of the details.

Head shape is important when showing
your hamster. The curve of the head from
nose tip to neck should be smooth.

be invaluable in respect to color breeding and, indeed, to breeding strategy in general.

OBTAINING INITIAL STOCK

It is crucial that you begin with stock whose color genes are known for sure. This will save a lot of wasted matings that produce colors that you may not want. Additionally, you need quality stock that is the result of planned breeding. This will greatly increase the chances that your breeding hamsters will produce offspring of at least their own worth, and hopefully better. Visit a few hamster shows if you can, and you will soon be chatting with the exhibitor/breeders. A little research will quickly establish which are long-time breeders of repute. Do not try and buy quality stock at a bargain price because you will basically get what you pay for.

Start with one male and two or three females from the same source. This will ensure that their breeding is compatible. Alternatively, you can ask the breeder to mate a female for you and agree to purchase two more mated females over the next couple of months, so your program gets underway without the initial need to have a male. This method works especially well if the breeder is in your locality.

BASIC FACTS ABOUT BREEDING

Breeding age: Although a female is capable of being mated as early as five weeks of age, this is certainly not advised. She should be physically mature before being bred, which means at least 12 weeks old. The male can likewise be bred at an early age but should be at least two months old before he is test mated. Always pair an unproven hamster of either sex to one that has proven itself.

Breeding condition: Never mate a hamster that is overweight, especially a female, as this could result in problems. The same is true of one that is not well or is recovering from an illness.

Breeding period: Hamsters will breed year 'round under controlled light and temperature conditions. It is best to restrict a female to no more than five litters per year. More than this is greedy and hardly gives the female time to rebuild her physical condition after the stress of birth and kit rearing.

Estrus cycle: Female hamsters come into breeding readiness (estrus) about every four days,

Hamsters will generally sniff one another before they begin to mate. It is imperative for a breeder to keep accurate records in order to produce properly bred animals.

and it lasts approximately 24-28 hours. Mating is best effected during the evening hours.

Mating: With hamsters, mating is perhaps comparable with the process in spiders! The larger female will not hesitate to attack her prospective partner if she is not in estrus. It is best to place her in the male's accommodations, where he will be more assertive, and she a little less so. However, monitor events and at the first sign of trouble remove her and try again the next evening, and so on until she accepts the male. This she will do by standing still with her tail raised so that he can mount her. He will mate her a number of times over a short period, after which she can be removed to her own accommodations.

Another method of introduction is to place each hamster in one half of a "honeymoon" cage (such as a small aquarium) divided with a mesh screen so that they can see and smell each other without being able to make contact. Once the female is seen to be interested in the male, you can lift the divider and hope matters will proceed as planned. If not, put them back into their own accommodations and try again another day.

Gestation: The time lapse between fertilization of the female's eggs and the birth of babies is 16-18 days, a very short period, indeed, for a mammal. The youngsters are born naked and blind, but within a few days they are fully furred. They commence eating solid foods within their first ten days.

This nest contains baby hamsters that are less than a week old. Hamsters can be kept with their mother until about four weeks of age at which time they must be removed or they could be attacked by their mother.

Hamsters get their coats about two weeks after birth. Then you will be able to distinguish various colors within the litter.

Litter size: The range is 1-16, but a typical litter will comprise 6-8. In large litters, the post-natal death rate will be higher than in smaller litters.

REARING

Hamsters have a tendency to be cannibalistic on their offspring if their environment is unstable. This comment covers a range of factors. If the female is undernourished, she may kill the babies, not basically for food, but because she instinctively knows that she cannot produce sufficient milk, nor provide enough food, to rear them. She may also kill them if they are deformed in any way.

If she is unduly disturbed by an overly inquisitive owner, this too can trigger protective cannibalism. The first-time mother may also cannibalize all or part of a litter because she becomes frightened or confused at the birth process. It is important that you establish why a female cannibalizes a litter. If this behavior is linked to a genetic trait, she must never be used again for breeding. You must first, however, ensure that all of the other reasons are not applicable before assuming the female has a genetic fault.

When the babies are about one month old, it is best to separate them into sex groups. By the age of eight weeks, the youngsters should ideally be placed into individual accommodations to remove the risk that they will start fighting. The female is capable of being mated at about the time that she weans the kits. In this trait, she differs from many other rodents that can conceive another litter within hours of giving birth to a litter.

It is never wise policy to remate your hamster as soon as the kits are weaned. Give her time to recover her full vigor—about four weeks is suggested. This gives a full breeding cycle as follows: gestation, 16 days; nursing, approximately 28 days; recuperation, 30 days.

BREEDING RECORDS

If you plan to breed on any kind of regular basis, it will be crucial that you keep detailed records of everything that transpires in your breeding room. The more detailed the records, the more useful they will be to you. Obviously you must balance this fact against your available time and inclinations. With this in mind, the following three sets of records represent minimum requirements.

1. Individual hamster record: This will contain the ID number of the hamster, identifying marks, color, birth date, sex, size, weight, and source. It will

Hamster babies are born blind and naked. After a week or so, you can begin feeding your newborns solid food.

This is a disaster waiting to happen. Every accommodation must be safe from an attack by another domestic pet. Cats are primary predators to your hamster.

record each mating in which the individual was involved (date, to whom) and the result (number of offspring). It will also record the genotype of the hamster if this information is known. Show wins can be noted on this record or listed in a separate register. The individual hamster record should also indicate longevity. It would also be useful to record the temperament of the hamster and the mothering ability in the case of females. A photograph would complete this record.

2. Breeding log: This document will record the hamsters used in any one mating (their number and color). It will record the date of mating, the date of births (thus the gestation period), the number of offspring, the number that died postnatally (and why, if known), colors, sexes, and weights at whatever date this can be effected.

3. Medical record: This will contain the ID number of each hamster that was ill, when the illness occurred, what the clinical signs were, what the diagnosis was, what the treatment was, and what the result was. Individual and multiple case histories can be very useful in tracking down weaknesses in your husbandry techniques, as well as potential genetic problems in the stock.

Before you make any attempt to breed hamsters, you may want to consider if you have the time and the environment to care for young hamsters. Remember, only one hamster to a cage.

Hamsters reproduce faster than any other mammal. Their gestation period is an average of 16 days.

EXHIBITION

The exhibition side of the hobby is a natural conclusion for any breeding program. It is the means by which you can assess how successful your breeding program is. At a show, the exhibits are entered into any of numerous appropriate classes. These classes may be based on age, sex, color, pattern, hair type, previous show wins or places, and on the exhibitor's status—adult or junior. The hamsters may be judged against a written standard, against each other, or a combination of both. Some shows are small local affairs; others are major open or national exhibitions where the best of the best compete.

Success at shows can significantly increase the value of your stock, but all competitors will gain something from exhibitions. This may be the social activity of meeting other breeders and, of course, the thrill of competition. What you should do is to make local inquiries to find out if there is a hamster or rodent club in your area. Upon joining such an organization, you will get much advice not only on how to prepare your pets but also on preparation of the show cage that you will need. The show cage must meet the criteria laid down by the national hamster club of your country, if there is one, or of the show organizers. Start by competing in the small shows and move up to the larger open shows based on your experience, confidence, and quality of stock.

HEALTH CARE

Hamsters are hardy little pets. But there are many problems and diseases that they can suffer from if their living conditions are allowed to deteriorate, if their nutrition is inadequate, or if you are not careful and inadvertently expose them to pathogens (disease-causing organisms).Taking these factors into consideration, your priorities are to:

1. Avoid problems and disease by correct husbandry techniques.
2. Recognize a hamster that is sick.
3. Take appropriate measures to isolate the unwell pet.
4. Diagnose the problem.
5. Treat the hamster.

In this short chapter, the legion of potential conditions and diseases cannot be discussed, so the advice is restricted essentially to a discussion of practical aspects of the priorities enumerated.

AVOIDING PROBLEMS—GENERAL HYGIENE

Although it may seem an overworked remark, the fact is that general hygiene really does make the difference between having many health-related problems and having few, if any.

The long-haired hamster varieties are generally not a wise choice for the novice pet owner, as they require more attention to coat care and cage cleanliness.

A young female gray satin. If a hamster is given clean surroundings and sufficient attention, your hamster will most likely remain very healthy throughout its life.

More diseases are transmitted due to lack of hygiene than via any other source, so let us recap what your husbandry priorities should be.

1. Clean the accommodations every single week—no misses. Do not forget the cage bars because your pet will often rub its snout on them—a very easy way to pick up germs.
2. Clean food pots every single day.

5. Wash your hands before and after handling your hamsters. Always handle unwell pets after you have completed your daily chores for other pets.
6. Breeders should ensure that their stock room is well ventilated but not drafty. Lack of fresh air is a major means of transmitting bacteria and allowing them to multiply.
7. Wear a nylon overall when working in the stockroom so

Hamsters have no known diseases of their own. They are hardy little creatures that can be raised with a minimum of trouble.

3. Breeders must ensure that the same pots and water dispensers go back to their respective cages.
4. Store all dry foods in a cool darkened cupboard that cannot be contaminated by mice. Store fresh foods in the refrigerator. Never feed any stale foods and always remove uneaten fresh foods within an hour or so.

that you minimize the risk of transferring pathogens from your clothes to your stock. This can happen after you have visited pet shops, veterinary clinics, hamster or other small mammal shows, or the breeding rooms of friends.
8. Maintain a constant temperature (within 2-4 degrees) in the room where your

Curing any kind of disease is difficult because most owners don't watch their pets closely enough to catch the disease at its onset. The best way to treat disease is to prevent it.

pet lives. The preferred range for hamsters is 65-80°F (18-26.7°C). For breeders, the relative humidity range is 40-70 percent in the stockroom. A level of about 50 percent is possibly ideal for hamsters.

RECOGNIZING THE ILL HAMSTER

It is possible that an ill pet will display no physical evidence of a problem until it dies! However, it may exhibit changes in its normal behavior patterns. You can pick up on these only if you have spent time observing your pet.

Changes to look for are: disinterest in food or water, especially if this extends to known favored items; excessive sleeping during periods when the hamster is normally quite active; sluggish movements and general lethargy; aggression in a normally docile individual when being handled; excessive scratching or biting of the fur; uncoordinated body movements—fits and their like; and excessive thirst. Any of these conditions are abnormal and do not occur unless there is a problem of a greater or lesser degree.

TAKE APPROPRIATE ACTION

Once you have determined that your pet is ill, you must not wait to see how things develop. Lost time can be fatal to a small animal like a hamster, which has a rapid metabolic rate. However, fast metabolism also means that such animals can make quite dramatic improvements in a short time if treatments are prompt and appropriate. Make notes on the clinical signs that your hamster is exhibiting. Note the state of its fecal matter if possible, and obtain a specimen for your vet to examine if required. Note the progression rate of the illness. Now phone your vet or take the pet to the clinic.

If this is not possible, for a day or two take the following measures. First, isolate the pet well away from other small animals. A breeder should have a commercial or homemade hospital cage in which the temperature is thermostatically controlled. The use of an infrared lamp is useful in the homemade unit.

Raise the ambient temperature to about 90°F (32°C). This alone may overcome minor chill-related problems. It can be 2-4 degrees higher, but the danger in small restricted cages is that the hamster may suffer from heat stress over a prolonged period. This is counterproductive to your objectives, so it is best to stay on the safe side.

If the pet's fecal matter is liquid, you should withhold moist foods (especially plant matter) until you can contact your vet. This will encourage the hamster to drink more water, which may be one of the ways in which a treatment may best be administered. Do bear in mind that when any animal has received short- or long-term heat treatment, it must be carefully acclimatized back to the temperature that it is normally accustomed to. The temperature should be reduced 1-2 degrees per day until it is at the normal heat level.

A healthy hamster will have bright eyes and a shiny coat. If your hamster appears to be getting sick, take it to the veterinarian immediately.

CORRECT DIAGNOSIS IS VITAL

Home diagnosis of anything but minor problems is fraught with danger. Many of the clinical signs of ill health are the same for a whole range of diseases, but the treatments for them can differ considerably. If the diagnosis is not accurate, then it is not possible to prescribe a course of

is well worth the cost because it may save all of the stock.

It should be mentioned that penicillins are known to be dangerous to hamsters, as are a number of antibiotics. The unqualified use of them is therefore very ill advised. If a hamster dies suddenly, the breeder should arrange for a

Most of the minor squabbles among hamsters involve food or a lack of personal space.

treatment. Often, microscopy of a blood sample, fecal matter, or a skin scraping is needed. Only your vet can attend to this need.

In the case of a pet, the cost of veterinary treatment will exceed the value of the hamster; but with a cherished pet, money should not be a consideration. With regard to the breeder, veterinary treatment

postmortem to try and establish the cause of death. At the same time, general hygiene should be rigidly rechecked.

TREATMENTS

There are many drugs now available for the treatment of small mammals, and it is also possible to conduct surgery on

Your hamster will only be as healthy as the food it eats. Remove any leftover food after four hours or so.

these pets. Whether either of these modes of treatment is cost justifiable can only be determined after consultation with your vet in light of the diagnosis. Medicine can be administered orally, by injection, or in the drinking water. The last method noted is the least reliable because it can be difficult to ensure that the needed dosage is taken. This having been said, it may often be the least problematic of the three options.

Cleanliness will go a long way in preventing any illnesses to your hamsters.

EXTERNAL PARASITES

Fleas and lice can be a problem for a pet living under dirty conditions—even more so for breeding females with litters. Fortunately, there are good treatments available from your vet. Repeat treatments will normally be needed to kill unhatched eggs that survive the first treatment. All bedding and floor covering must be destroyed and replaced. Be sure to inspect your pet on a regular basis for external parasites.

HIBERNATION

Hamsters may hibernate under the following conditions: when the temperature drops below the normal range; when the hamster is able to store large quantities of food; when it is housed in deep litter that is not replaced on a regular basis; and when the pet is infrequently handled. When it is in a torpid state, you could think that the pet has died or is seriously ill. I am sure that you will not let these conditions prevail. But if, perchance, your pet does become exposed to a major drop in temperature, you should slowly return the heat level a few degrees each day until activity is restored.

WOUNDS

Small cuts or wounds should first be carefully cleaned with tepid water. Then an antiseptic lotion or cream should be applied to the wound to safeguard it from secondary infection while it heals. Major wounds must be treated by your vet as quickly as possible, or death through blood loss or resultant infection may well be the result.

If you diligently follow the advice given in this chapter, your pet hamster will indeed be very unfortunate if it should suffer from any major disease. The chances are high that it will live a happy and healthy life.

A fit youngster will be constantly inquisitive and on the move.

WHICH VARIETY?

In this chapter, the many varieties of hamster are presented in a simple overview. Hamsters can be conveniently divided into two color groups: the solid colored and the patterned. Then there are the four coat types: the normal, the satin, the long-haired, and the rex.

The coat types are available in any of the colors or patterns; thus, the total potential range is considerable. Some of these varieties may be extremely difficult to obtain. Brief mention is also given to other species of hamsters, some of which are already gaining a degree of popularity.

SOLID-COLORED HAMSTERS

ALBINO: There are two so-called albinos in the hamster, by which is meant that they are not full albinos by definition. One is the dark-eared albino; the other is a synthetic created by combining the dark-eared with another mutation. The latter is usually one that is itself a reduced pigment mutation, e.g., cinnamon. The dark-eared variety develops pigment in its ears, commencing when it is about one month old. Later, pigment forms around the genitals. The dark-eared could thus be regarded as an incomplete Himalayan.

Hamsters come in different sizes, coats, colors and patterns.

The color of a hamster has little to do with its behavior. This is a cream hamster. This variety can have either black or red eyes.

WHITE: There is a black-eyed white variety that is very pleasing. However, the genetic base of the color is anomalous and results in a percentage of either eyeless or rudimentary-eyed individuals if black-eyed whites are paired together. With this in mind, the black-eyed white should always be bred to non-black-eyed whites so that the anomalous genes are never in double dose.

CREAMS: There are a number of creams, which range from extremely light, almost blond, to quite dark. They are the black-eyed, the ruby-eyed, and the red-eyed. Each differs in the shade of cream, with the ears ranging from black to brown, depending on the mutant genes present.

BLOND, CINNAMON, AND RUST: These are all variations on the basic golden color. The blond is a yellow tone. The cinnamon is a light brown. The rust is a darker brown. In these varieties, the black hairs are reduced to browns. There are black and red-eyed forms.

GRAYS: There are light grays and dark grays, the latter probably being the more popular as they display less brown in their fur. The light gray is based on a lethal gene, meaning that in double dose the embryos die prenatally. The only effect of this from a breeding viewpoint is that litter size is reduced. Dark grays have a tendency to produce smaller offspring, so it is advised

A male blonde hamster.

that they are bred back to normals that are carrying the dark gray gene.

LILAC AND DOVE: These are more recent colors created by pairing the dark gray with the cinnamon (to produce lilac) or with rust (to produce dove). They are delicate and pleasing shades.

SMOKE PEARL: Combining the dark gray and cream mutations creates the very attractive smoke pearl, which has black (or very dark) ears and eyes contrasting against a grayish-fawn body color. It can also be produced by pairing the dark gray with the honey.

BLACK: The black may be compared with the albino in the hamster in that it is not a true black from a genetic standpoint. The responsible gene, known as umbrous, darkens the normal golden color. An almost black appearance can be obtained by pairing this mutant with cream, while chocolates are created if the mutant is combined with cream

A female cinnamon satin. Satin coats are fine and silky with a very characteristic gloss.

A light smoke pearl hamster eating a nutritious meal.

and rust. A truer description of the color would probably be sable, as there is a light eye ring and lighter underbelly color.

Other colors, such as the red-eyed caramel, are always being developed. Do understand that very often the color name applied to a hamster variety is often less striking when seen "in the flesh" than how it sounds from the name applied to it, sometimes by very enthusiastic breeders! Also, the name given to a particular color can vary from one region to another, and more so from one country to another.

From the colors discussed, it can be appreciated that the serious hobby breeder really does need to have a basic understanding of genetics if problems are to be avoided and objectives are to be achieved in the breeding room.

COLOR PATTERNS

PIEBALD: This pattern comprises patches of white and color. There are two forms recognized, one being called piebald, and the other known as dominant spot. Visually, the two forms look much the same, but they are created by different mutations that express themselves very differently, other than by their color. When two mutations display similar outward expressions, they are

Your local pet shop will have a wide selection of hamsters to choose from. Do not overlook certain considerations that you must go through before making an investment.

Your hamster's face should be short and blunt with the ears and nose forming an equilateral triangle. The length of the head should not exceed the distance between the ears.

A black hamster. This is one of the newer varieties that is becoming popular with owners.

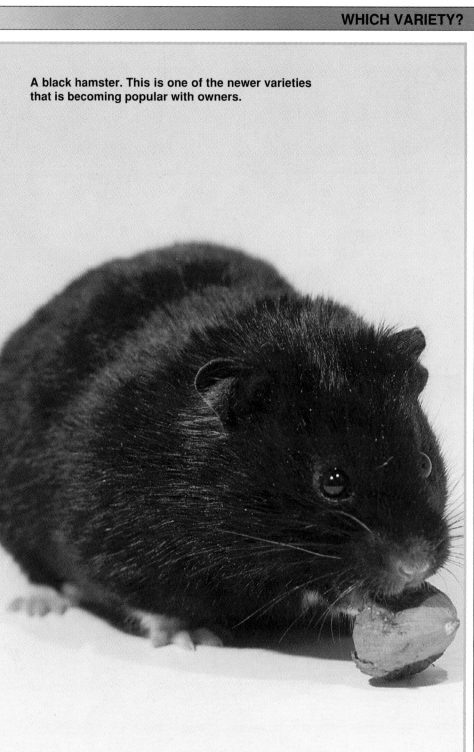

A mink hamster. If you looking for a hamster as a pet, rather than to breed, you should look into buying a strong and well-developed youngster.

known as mimic genes; and they can create confusion for breeders.

The pattern can range from extremely beautiful to rather nondescript. Unfortunately, there is a large element of luck involved in what kind of stock a breeder produces, because the pattern is not under breeder control. It can range from a few isolated small patches of white on a colored background, to an almost white hamster with a few patches of color on the body. Further, the white may mix with color to produce a brindled effect.

The piebald tends to be rather smaller than the normal hamster, has a reputation for being more aggressive, is associated with pre- and postnatal deaths, and its mothering instincts are lower than with other varieties. These drawbacks have made the variety rather scarce in recent years, though the pattern is arguably better than in its dominant spot counterpart. The latter, other than being a little smaller than the normal hamster, is otherwise free of the drawbacks exhibited by the piebald.

However, the dominant spot is an obligate heterozygote, which means that when two examples are bred, 25 percent of their offspring will die prenatally. This reduces litter size expectations and produces both spotted individuals and normal-colored hamsters in the theoretical ratio of 2:1. If you possess two white marked hamsters and they produce any normal colored individuals, this tells you that the parents are in fact dominant spots, not the piebald variety. These aspects aside, the spotted hamsters are always well liked if they are of a nice pattern.

It must be stated that some breeders, through lack of knowledge more than anything else, have bred black-eyed whites to either of the patterned varieties in order to increase the extent of white patches. When the offspring of these matings are bred together, the result is a percentage of eyeless or rudimentary-eyed offspring. The problem this creates is that the piebald can be condemned for something (the eye problem) that it is not in fact related to. The moral of this is that you should never jump to conclusions over traits and features perceived to be linked to colors (or other features) unless there is well-studied and documented evidence that this is so.

WHITE BANDED: Like the piebald, this pattern is also very variable in its expression. Ideally, the band should be even and encircle the entire body. Its edges should not intrude on the adjacent fur. Alas, most examples fall short of the ideal exhibition requirements, so it is a frustrating pattern for the breeder/exhibitor, with many individuals being only of pet quality. These, however, can be very attractive. The breeder of banded hamsters should retain only those displaying the best banding. By this process, it is possible to increase the number of nicely marked examples. By combining the banded mutation with

Water is best given in the drinking bottles that are sold in pet shops. These are inexpensive and there are many to select from.

Dominant spot you could, in theory, produce another version of Black-eyed white—once again by retaining only those examples displaying maximum white.

TORTOISESHELL AND WHITE: This is another pattern that displays great variability. The basic requirement is that there be patches of color, yellow, and white. Ideally, the patches should be distinct. The tortoiseshell and white is an unusual mutation because it is sex linked. This means that all torties are in fact females. The pattern is always very popular with both pet owners and exhibitors.

COAT TYPES

NORMAL: The fur is short and moderately glossy.

SATIN: This coat type has a very high gloss to it. The color of any hamster with a satin coat will be a little darker when compared to the same color in the normal coat. In the long-haired (Angora) variety, the reverse will be true. The mutant gene that creates the satin is an example of semi-dominance. This means that when it is in single dose, the most desirable satin is created. When it is in double dose, the result is that the fur is thinner and less neat—it is known as ultra-satin, but it has no more sheen than the regular satin. It is best to avoid satin-to-satin matings: pair your satin to a normal to avoid the appearance of ultra-satins.

LONG-HAIRED (ANGORA): This coat type is known as the Teddy in the US. It is seen at its best in the male and in the self

There are grooming tools specially designed for small animals such as hamsters. Regularly grooming your pet will help to keep its coat looking nice and healthy. Photo courtesy of Four Paws.

(one color) varieties. It takes a few months for the full length of the coat to grow. The ideal coat will have good density, not just excessive length. The responsible mutant gene acts in a simple recessive manner, which means that it must be in double dose to be expressed. If a long-haired is mated to a normal, the result will be all normal-haired individuals, but all of them will be carrying the long-haired gene. If they are mated to hamsters of a similar genotype, the expectations will be 1:2:1 of long-haired, normals carrying the long-haired gene, and normals, which will have no long-

A female golden satin hamster. This is a very popular color variety.

haired genes in their make-up. Unfortunately, you cannot visually distinguish between a normal and a normal carrying the long-haired gene, so genotype will have to be established based upon breeding results. Of course, long-haired mated to long-haired will produce 100 percent long-haired offspring.

It is very important that if you keep longhaired hamsters, you are prepared to devote much time to gentle grooming. The long-haired is really not a variety suited to the average person; it is better kept by the breeder/exhibitor who is prepared to make the commitment to grooming that it requires.

REX: The effect of this mutation is that the guard hairs are shorter and crinkled, as is the undercoat, but to a lesser degree. The whiskers are also crinkled. The mutation is seen at its best in rabbits. One day it may reach this level of quality in the hamster.

The desired objective is that the coat looks like velvet. To achieve this, it is important that only those individuals with the densest hair should be used for breeding; otherwise, the rex mutation can result in a coat that is sparse and not especially impressive. Like the long-haired, the rex mutation is inherited as a simple recessive.

You can combine any of the coat mutations in the same hamster, because each of them is inherited independently of the others. However, when this is done the results are rarely very successful. You end up with something that is a combination of the mutations. Sometimes this can produce a nice effect. The down side is that before achieving this to any constant degree, you will most certainly produce many inferior-coated individuals. Such matings are therefore best left to the specialist who knows what he is doing and is prepared to pursue that objective over many carefully documented generations.

OTHER HAMSTER SPECIES

DESERT, OR DWARF, HAMSTER: *Phodopus sungorus.* This little hamster is indigenous to Mongolia, Manchuria, Siberia, and many parts of China. Its average length is only about 10cm (4 in.), plus a short tail. It is a cute little animal with large eyes and relatively large ears, reflecting its desert homelands (the ears dissipate heat). The upper-body parts are a gray-pink; the underbelly is white or gray. The muzzle, cheeks, and an area above the eyes are white. The silky coat is somewhat longer than in the wild-type golden hamster, which it is easily distinguished from by size and general appearance. A dark dorsal stripe may be present. The species is easily tamed and makes a good pet. The gestation period is 18-19 days, and the litter range is 1-9, with 4-5 being typical. The female has eight mammae. Longevity may well exceed that of the golden hamster. It has the potential to be a very popular species with the hamster specialist.

BLACK-BELLIED, OR COMMON, HAMSTER: *Cricetus cricetus.* Indigenous from Europe to Siberia, there are many subspecies of this hamster. Some authorities include the golden hamster within the genus. It is a little larger than the golden, which it otherwise resembles in general appearance. The typical color pattern is a medium to light brown on the back, black on the underparts, with white under the chin and on the cheeks. There are also vertical white patches on either side of the front legs. However, color is very variable and ranges from almost albino to melanistic (black). Unlike the golden hamster, the common hamster is somewhat more social with its own kind. Pairs have remained together and reared young under captive conditions. Likewise, family colonies have been reported, but neither of these situations are typical in the wild and should only be attempted with great caution.

The gestation period is 18-20 days, and the litter range is 2-12 days, with 4-6 probably being typical. The female has eight mammae, and the youngsters reach sexual maturity when they are about six weeks old. Full physical maturity is not attained until at least eight weeks of age. Longevity is in the range of two to two-and-one-half years, thus comparable with the golden. The species, especially those displaying much black underbelly fur, should prove popular with hamsterophiles.

RATLIKE HAMSTER: Genus *Cricetulus*. There are 12 species in this genus, and their range is much the same as for the common hamster. In size, they may be smaller than the golden, or larger, and the tail is somewhat longer. The basic color pattern is gray agouti with white underparts, feet, and tail tip. Gestation period is 17-22 days, and the litter range is 2-12, with 5-6 being typical. The female has eight mammae. A number of the species have a reputation for being rather aggressive with their own kind,

A female cinnamon Russian dwarf. When your hamster has awakened from its sleep, it is best to leave him be for a few minutes before you play with your pet.

and humans alike. Others have been kept in captivity and compare favorably with other hamsters.

A male Chinese hamster.

MOUSELIKE HAMSTER:
Calomyscus bailwardi. This species is included here only because it is presently classified as a close relative of the hamster. It is small (mouse size) and sports a fur-tipped tail that is normally longer than the body. The ears are large, and it displays the appearance more of a jerboa than of a hamster, so it is not likely to appeal to the true hamster enthusiast.

A normal hamster cage with bars cannot be used for dwarf hamsters because they can squeeze through the bars. An aquarium tank—pictured here—is more appropriate.

PRIMER

Common name: Golden, or Syrian, hamster.

Scientific name: *Mesocricetus auratus.*

Head-body length: Approximately 13-15cm (5-6 in.).

Tail length: 1.2cm (under 1/2 in.).

Distribution: Restricted to Mount Aleppo region, NW Syria.

Number of varieties: Over 120, including coat types of normal, satin, long-haired, and rex.

Longevity: Two years or a little more.

Sex differences: Females have mammae and are often larger. The ano-genital distance is greater in the male than in the female.

Compatibility: Solitary and best kept in separate housing.

Physical maturity: Approximately eight weeks or a little more.

Breeding age: 12 weeks or older is earliest advised.

Gestation period: 16-18 days.

Number of mammae: 12-17; Other hamster genera have only 8.

Litter size: 1-16; 6-8 typical.

Weaning: About 21 days.

Best purchase age: About 30 days or over.

Litters per year: Five suggested to allow female to recoup between litters.

Diet: Omnivorous. Grain, seeds, vegetables, fruit, and other plant matter, together with cheese, boiled egg, and some meat; may take invertebrates.

Major diseases: Wet tail (an acute diarrhea) and pneumonia. Sound and regular hygiene is the key to maintaining good health.